The Dick Ways

Phenomenal Swear Word To Color

For Stress Releasing

J.N. Moorcroft

I0463321

Happy Coloring!

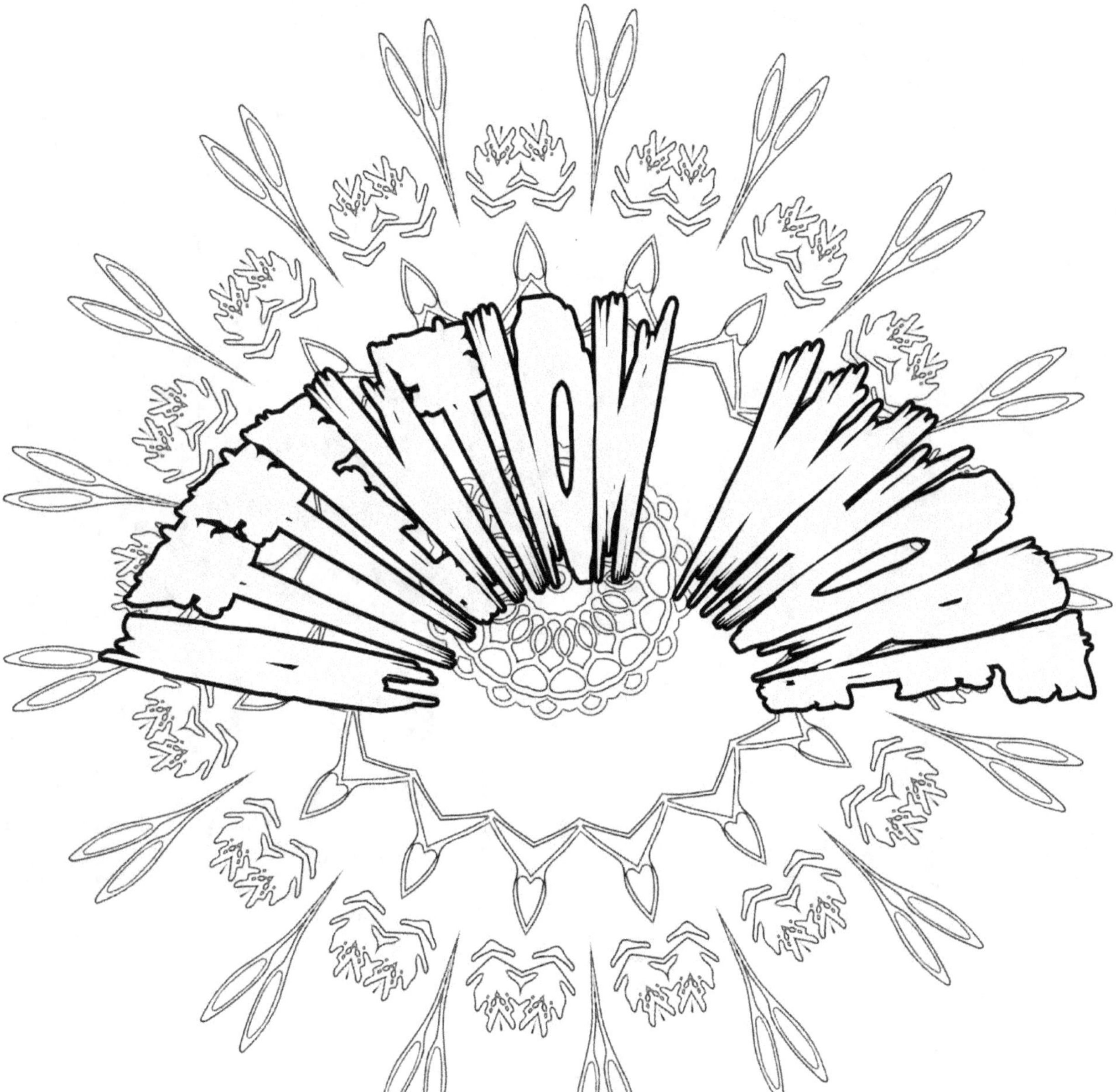

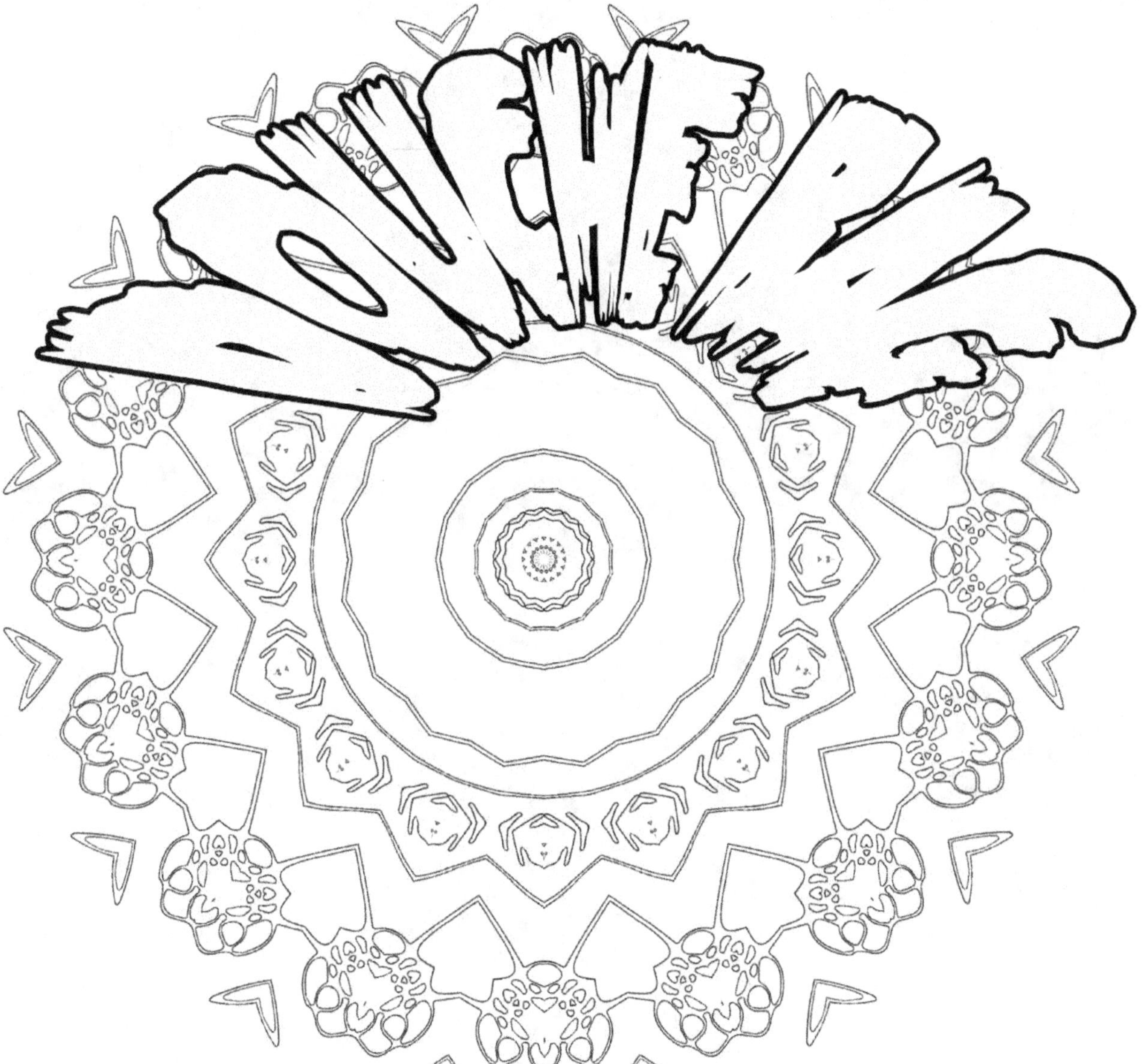

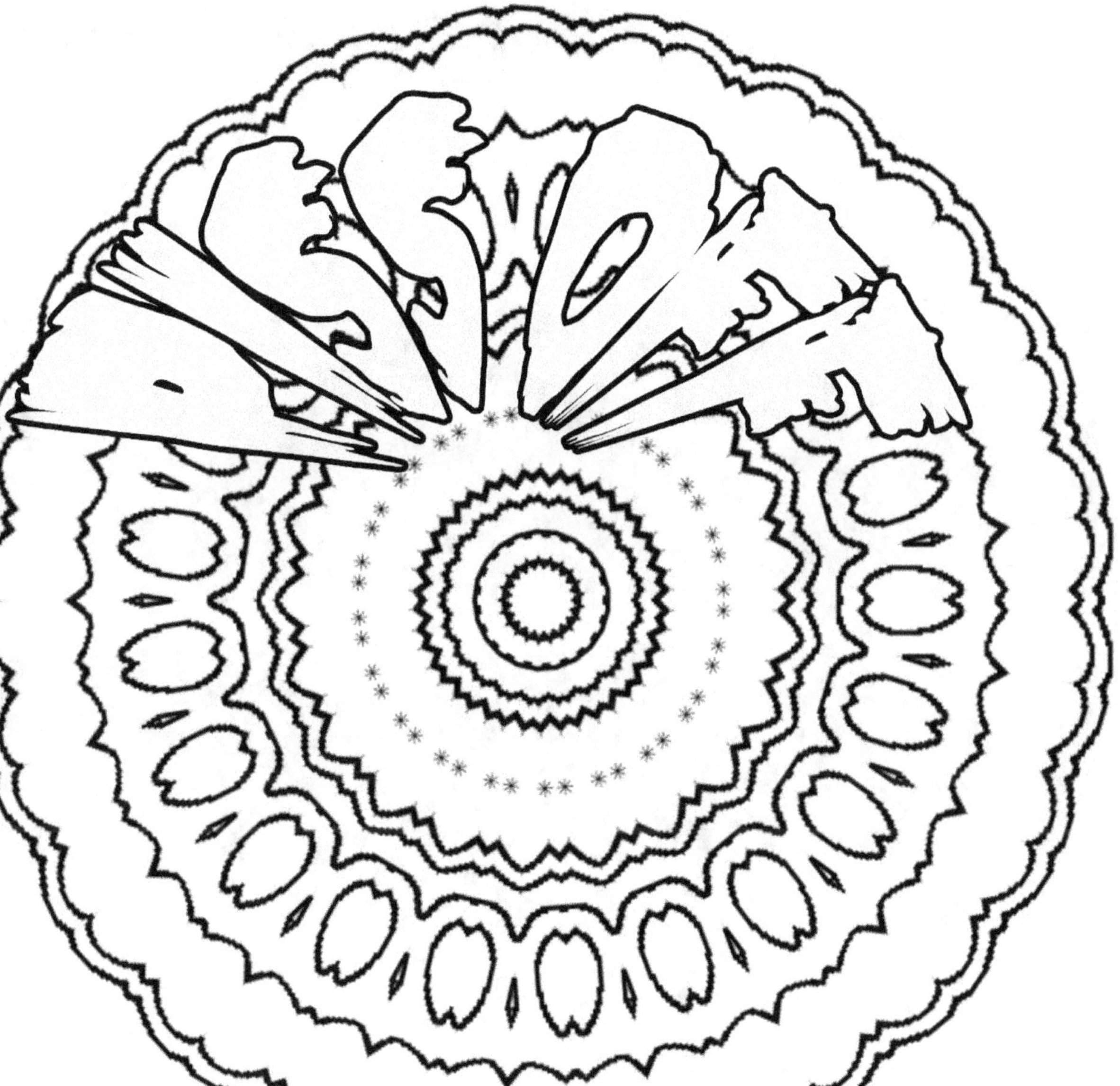

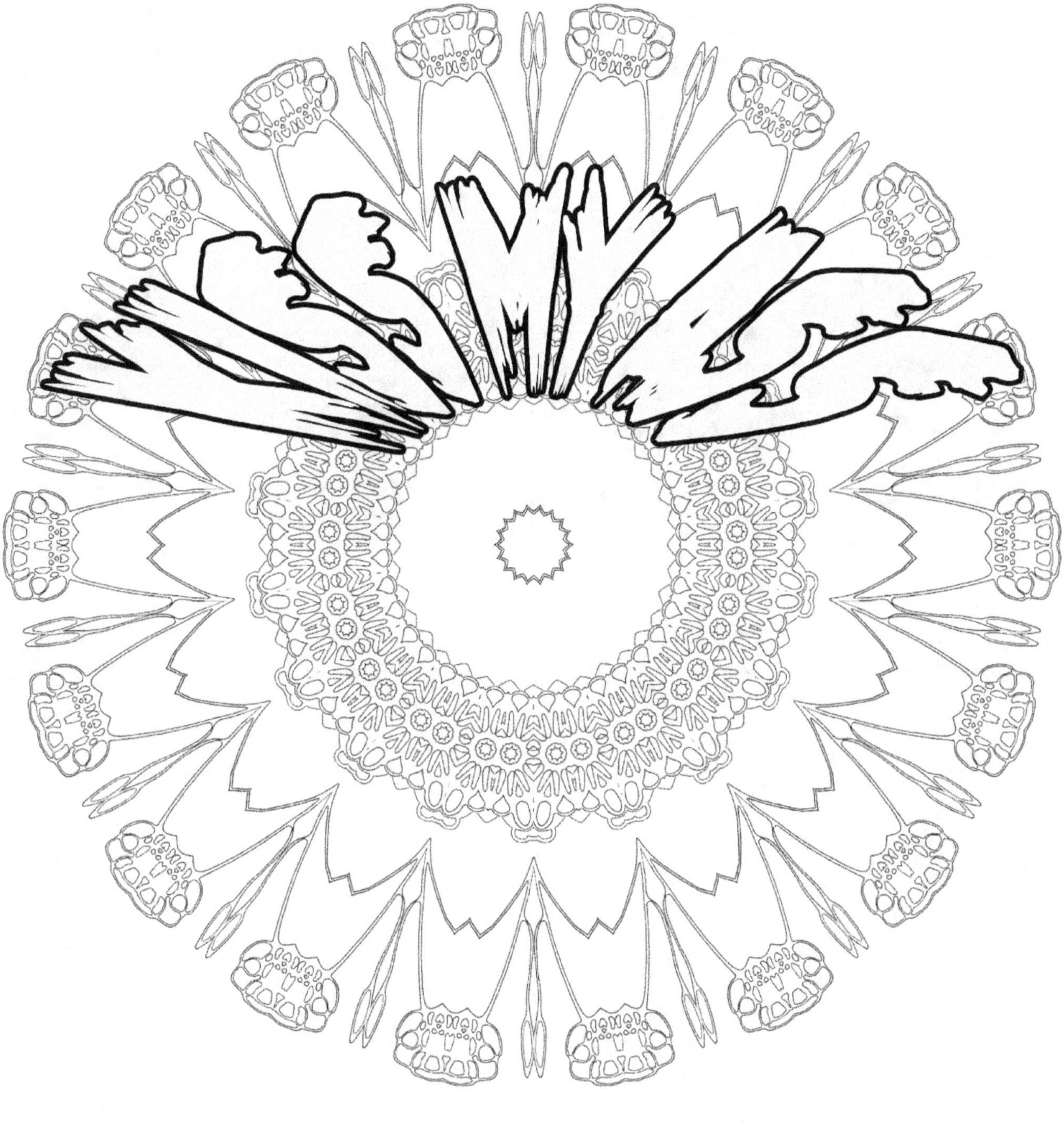

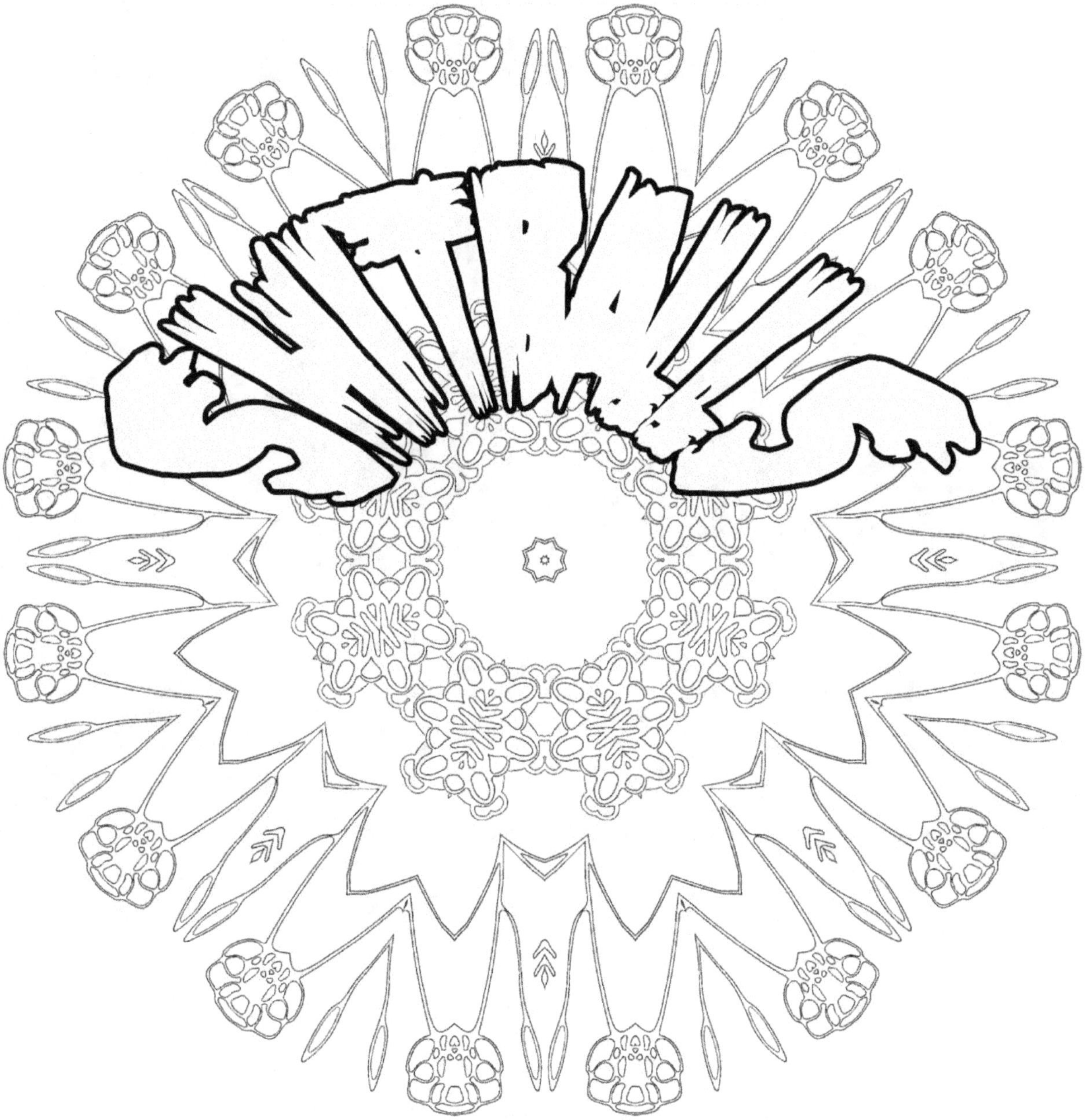

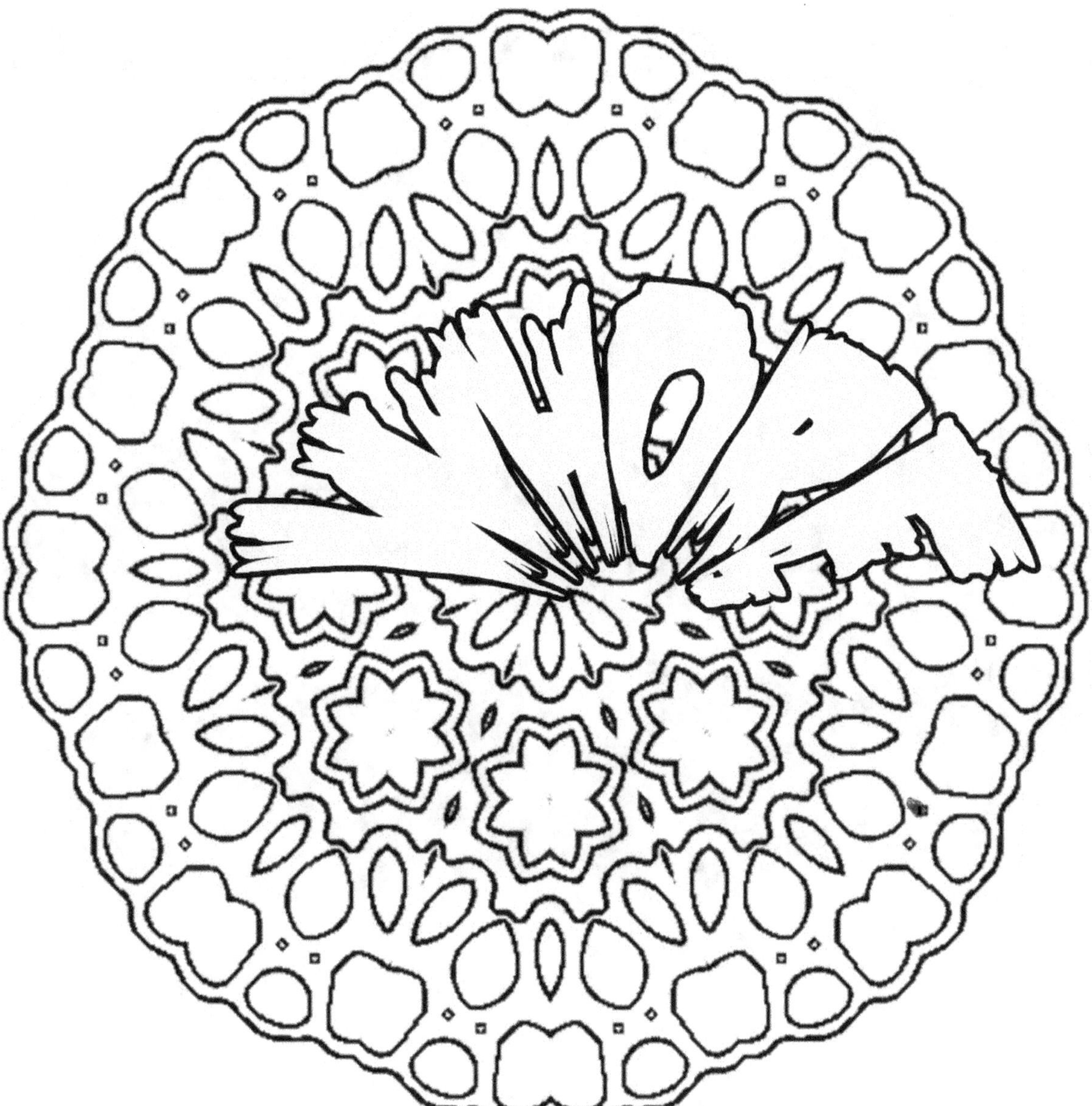

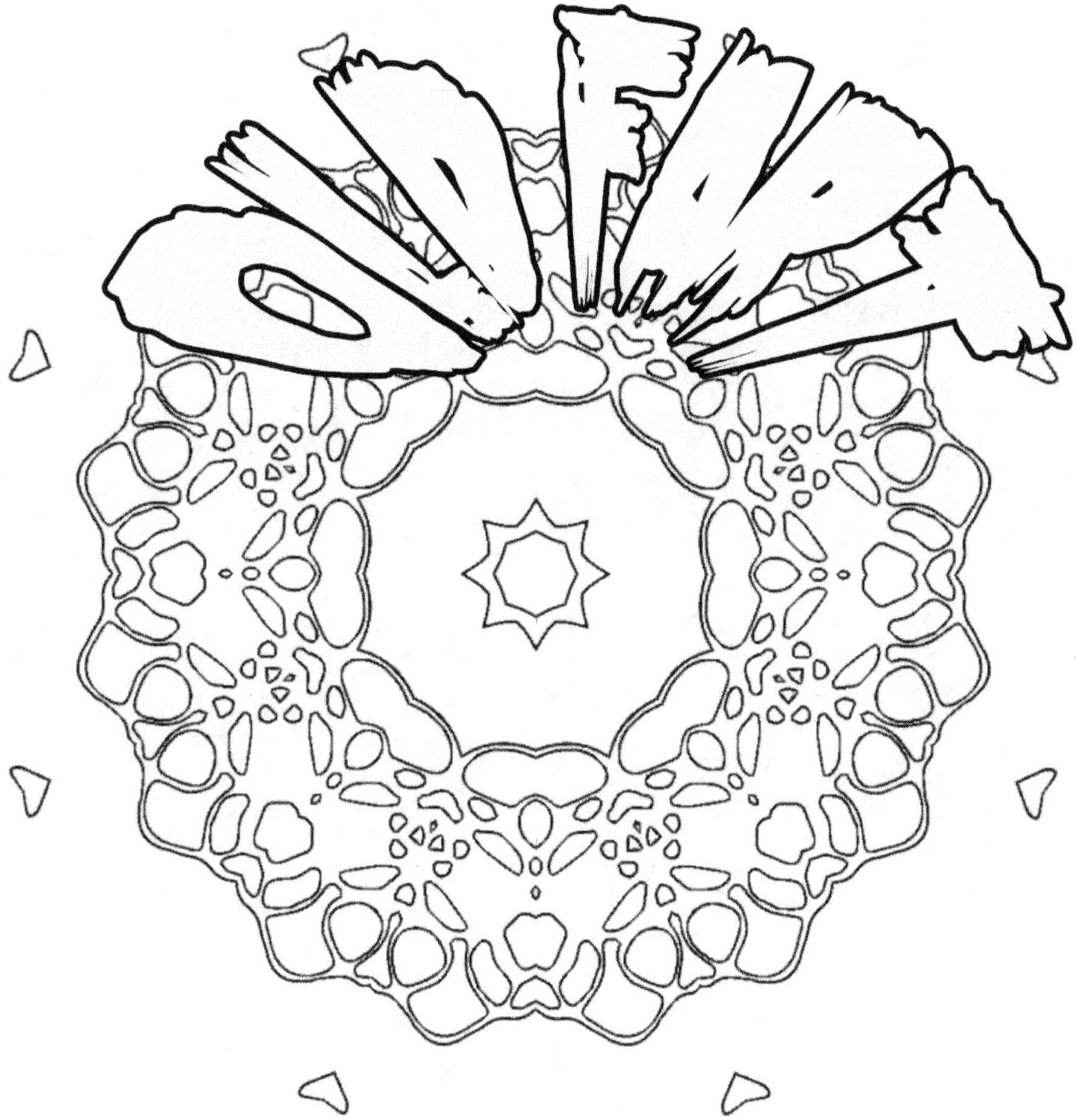

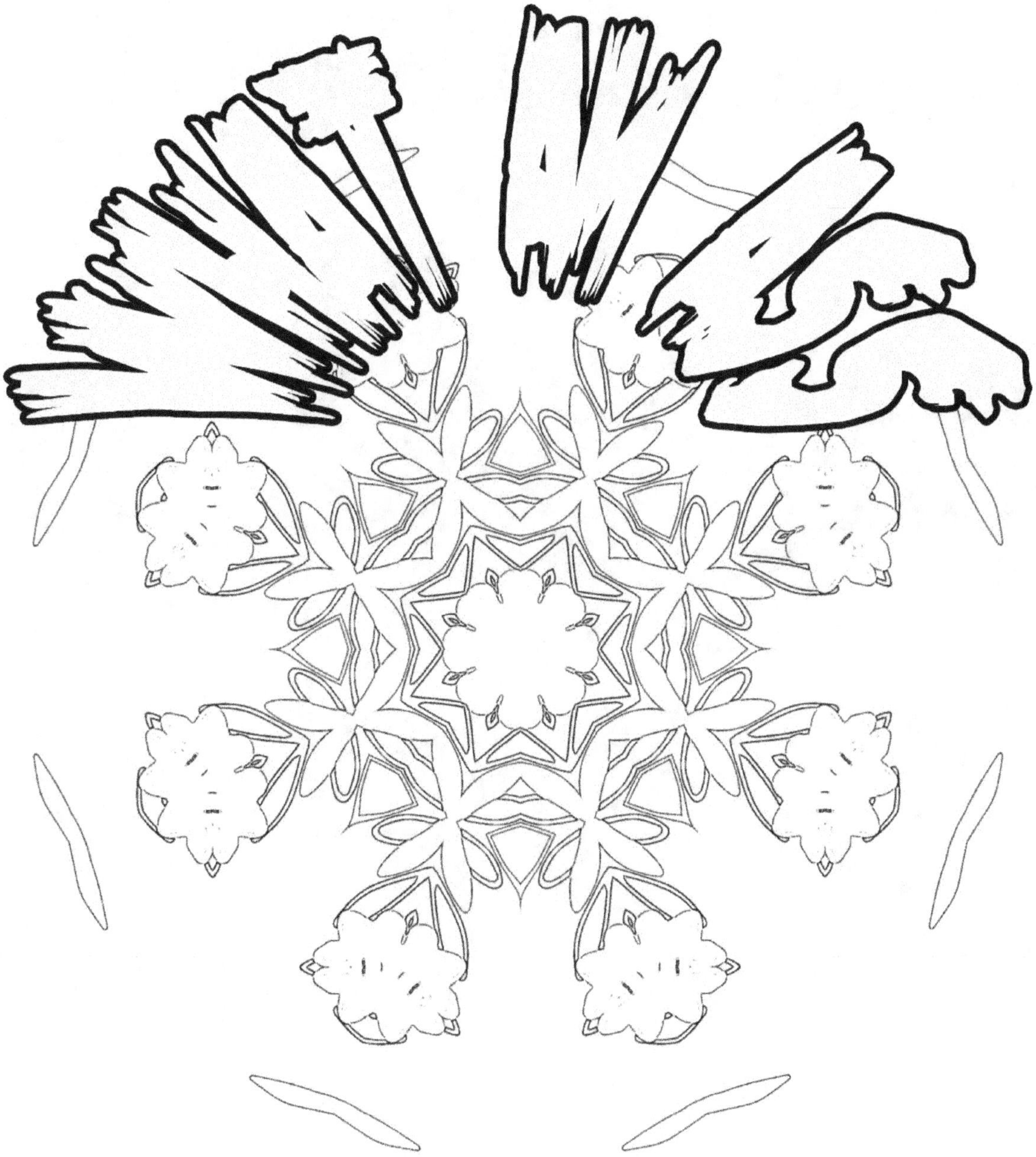

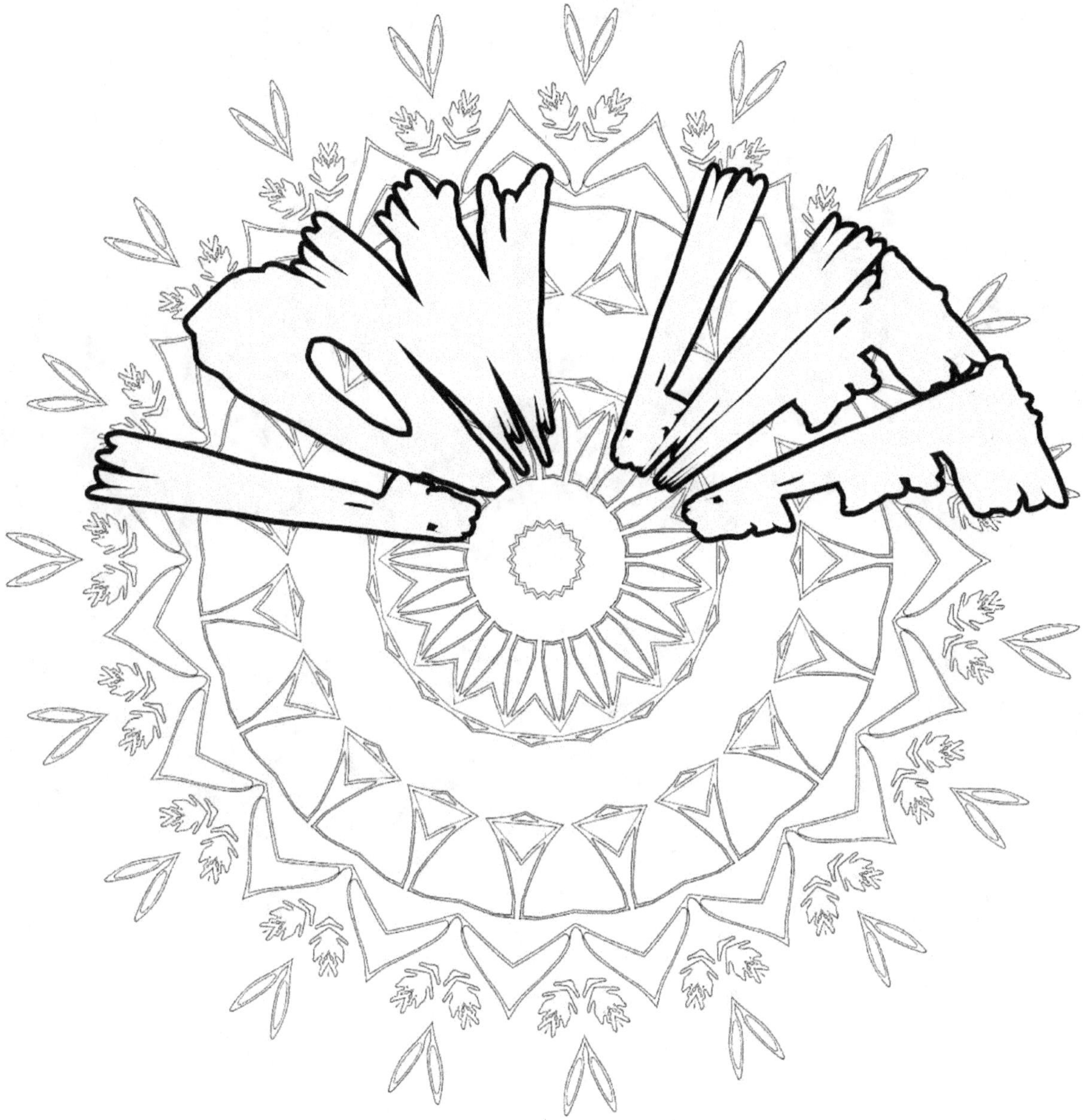

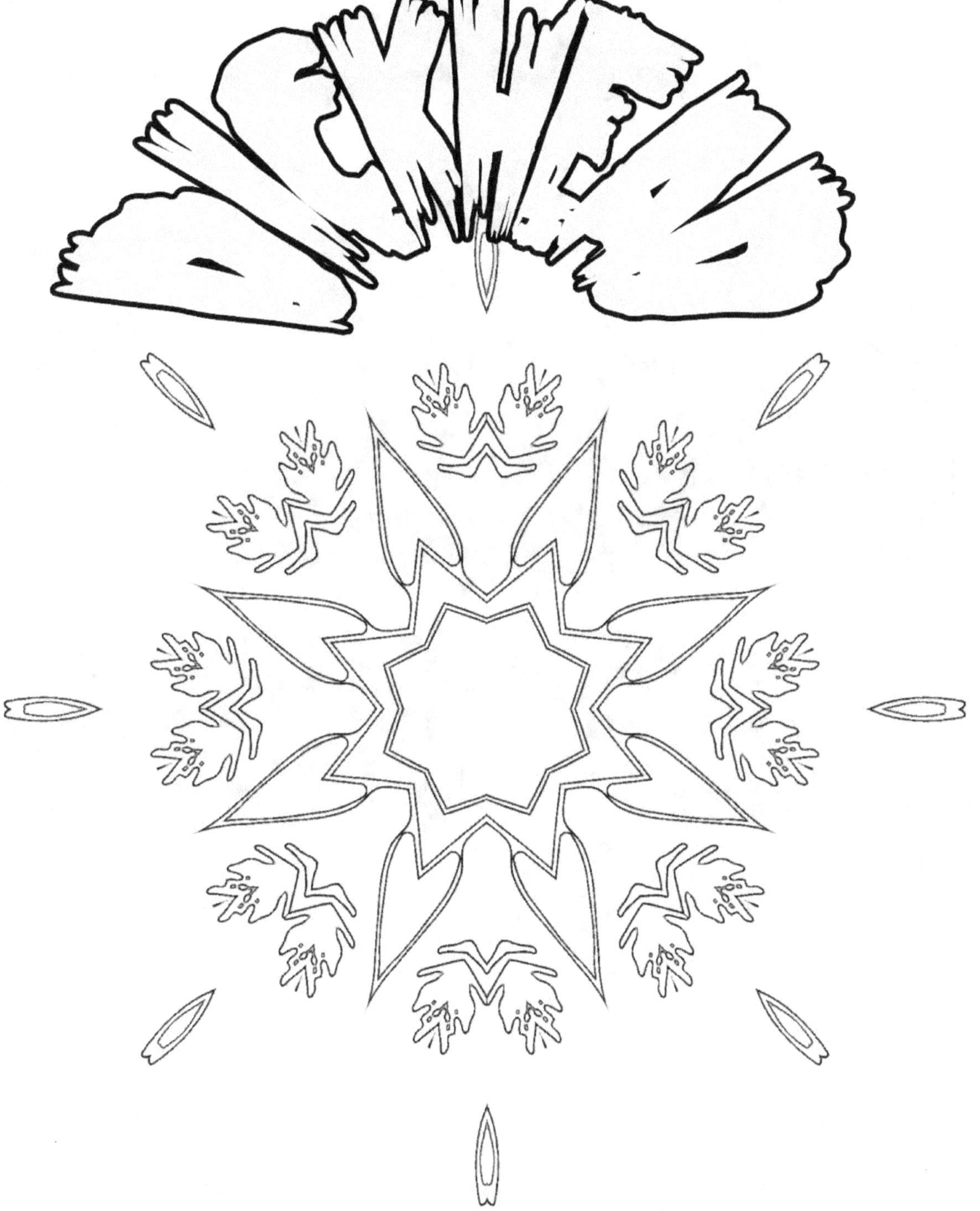
DICKHEAD

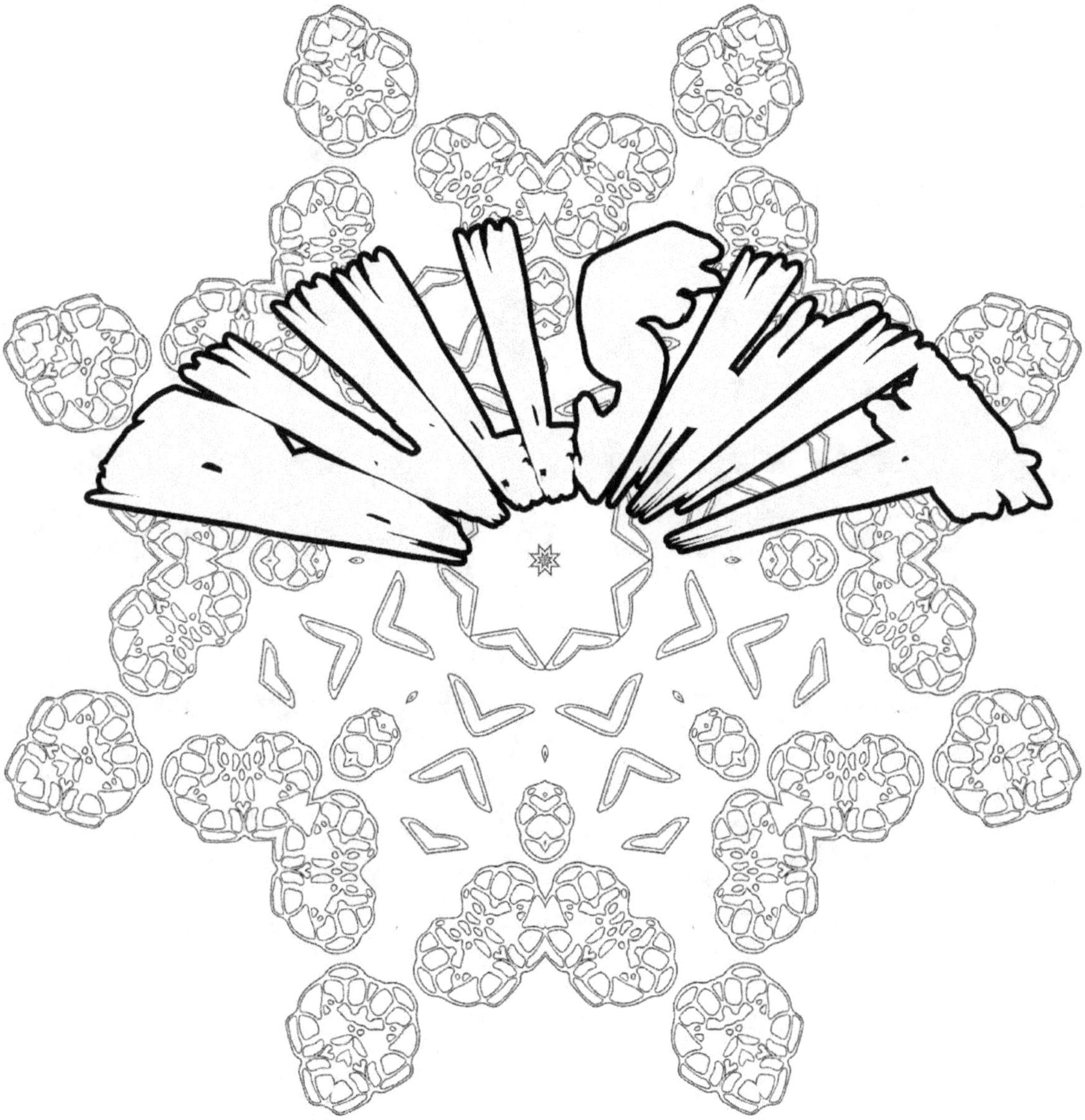

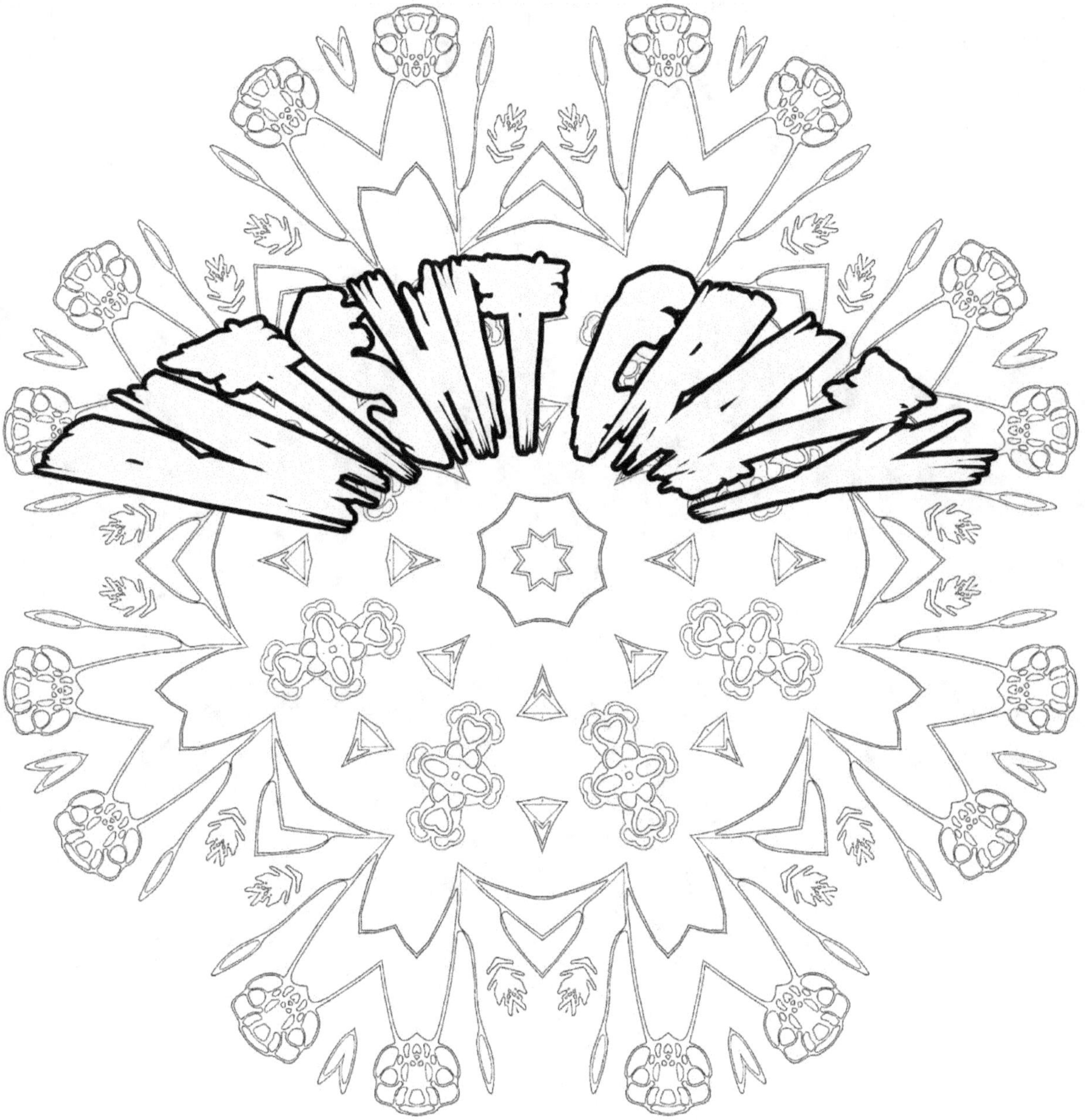

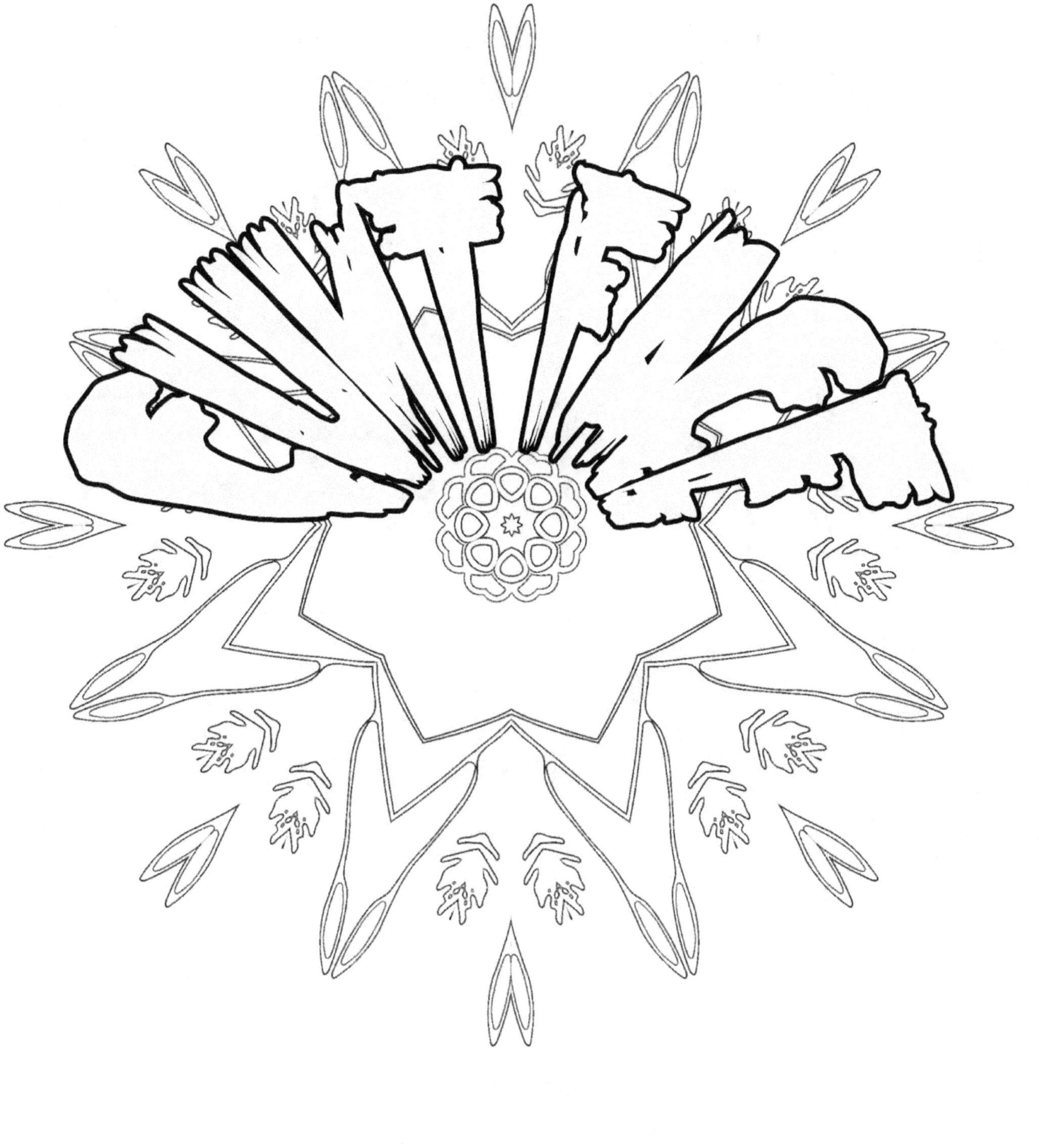

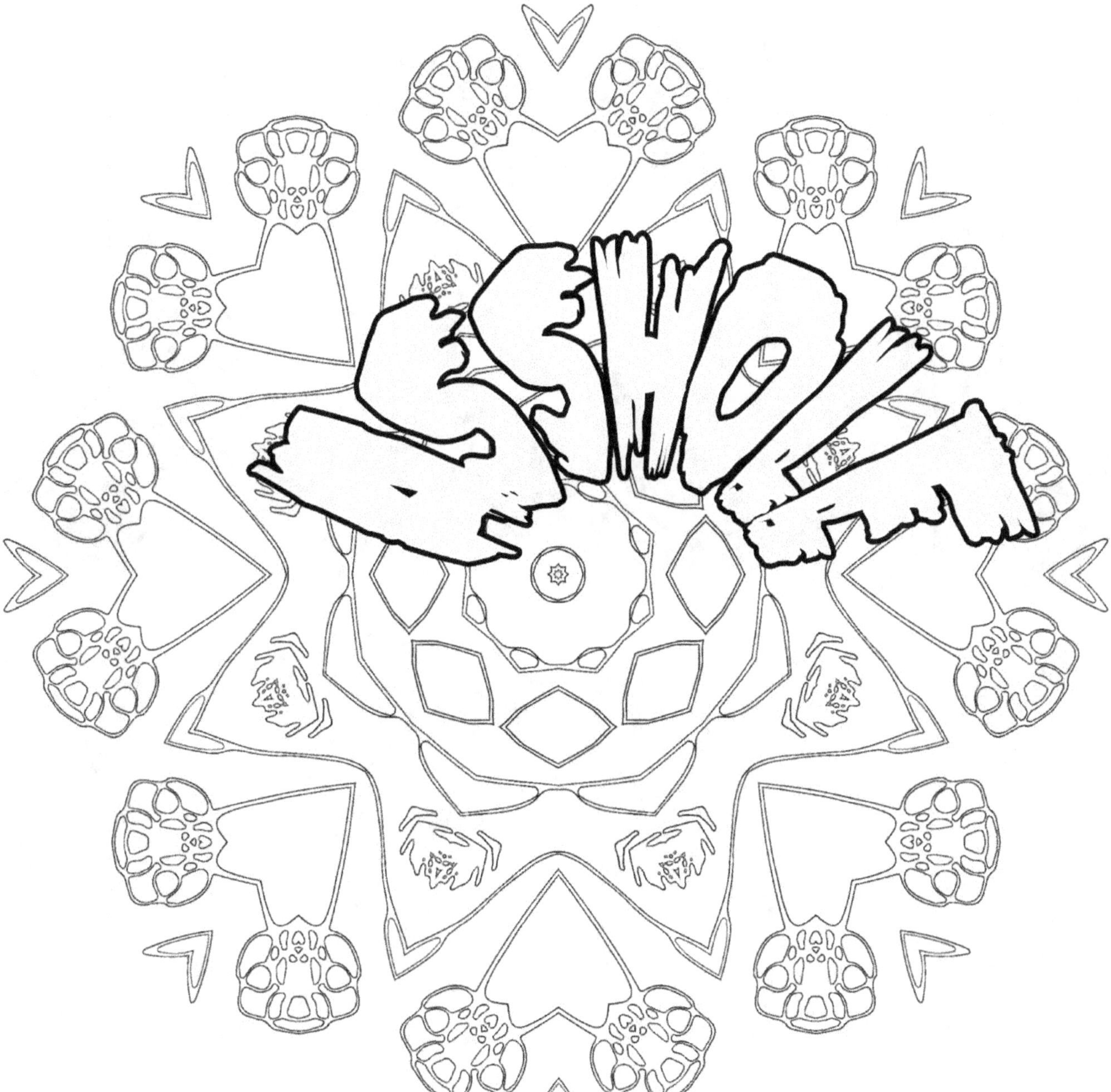
ASSHOLE

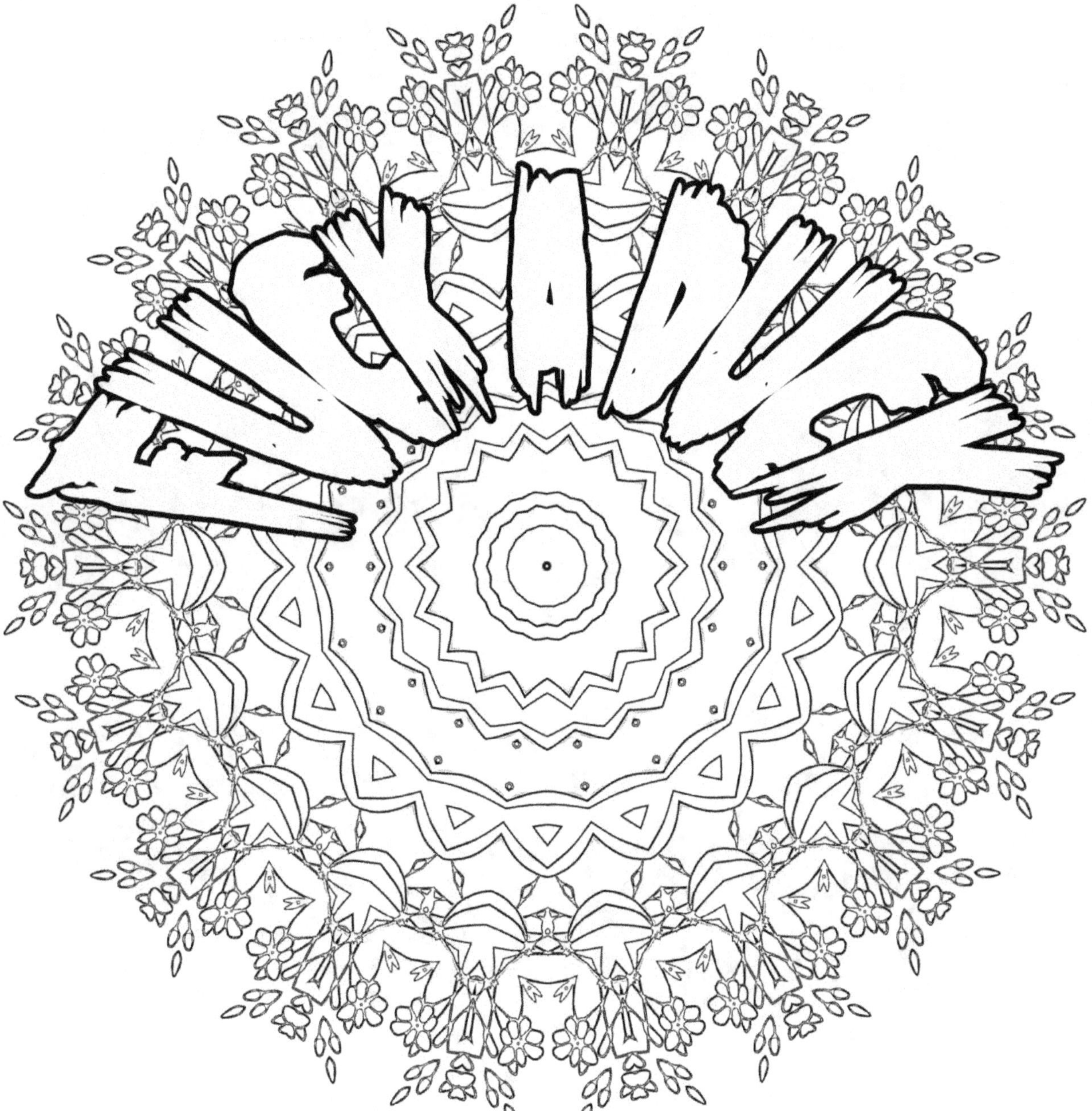

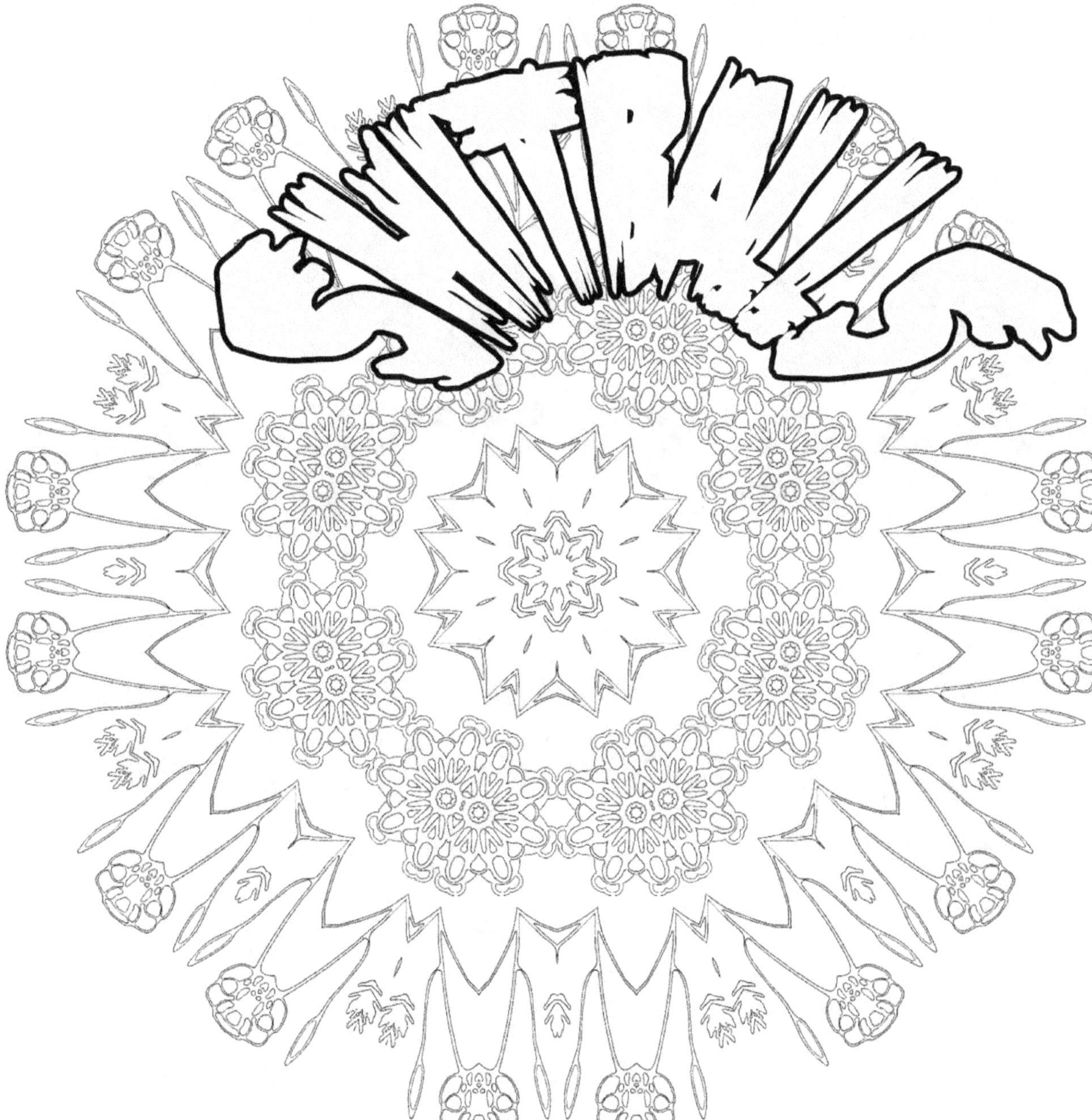

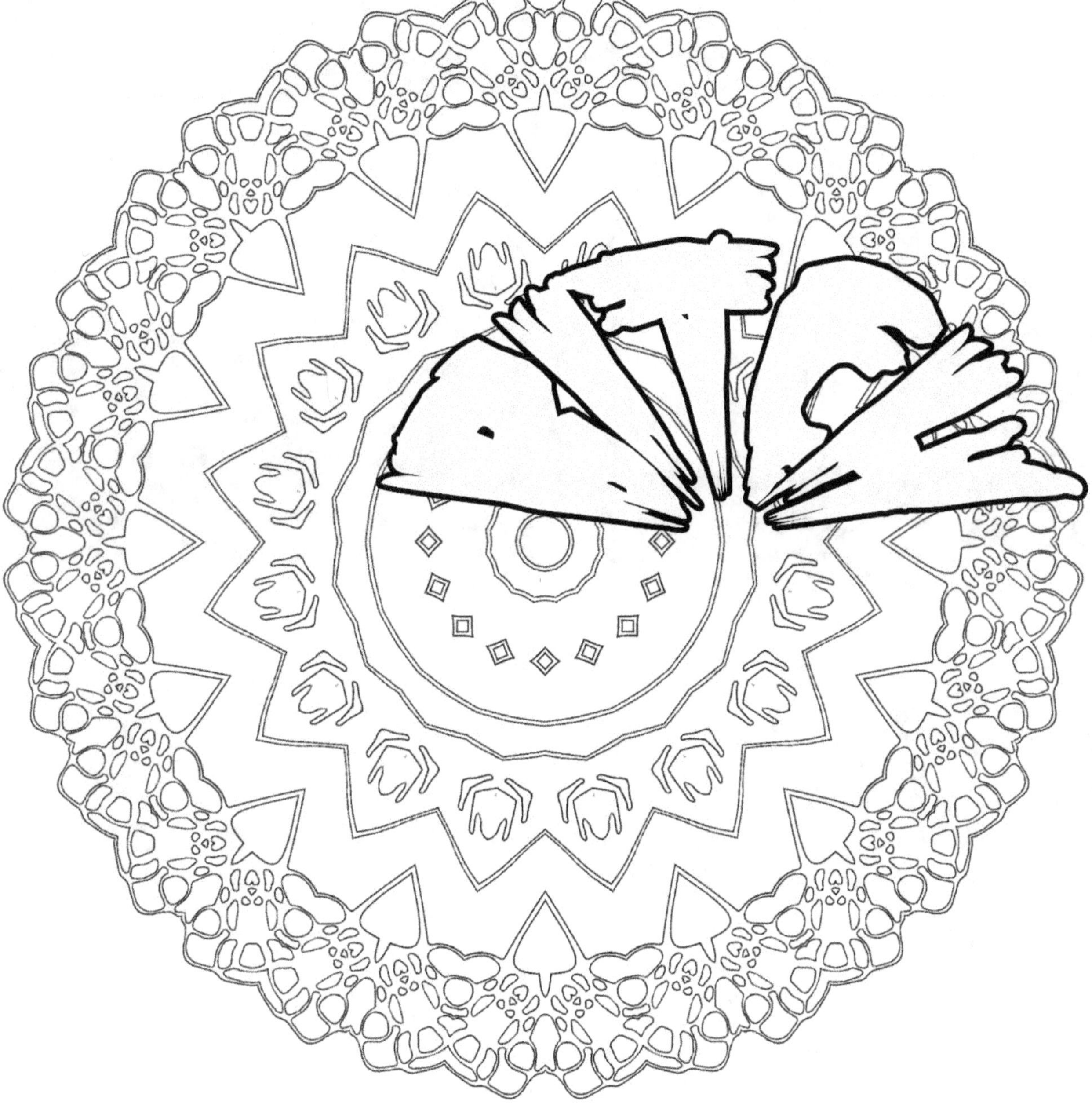

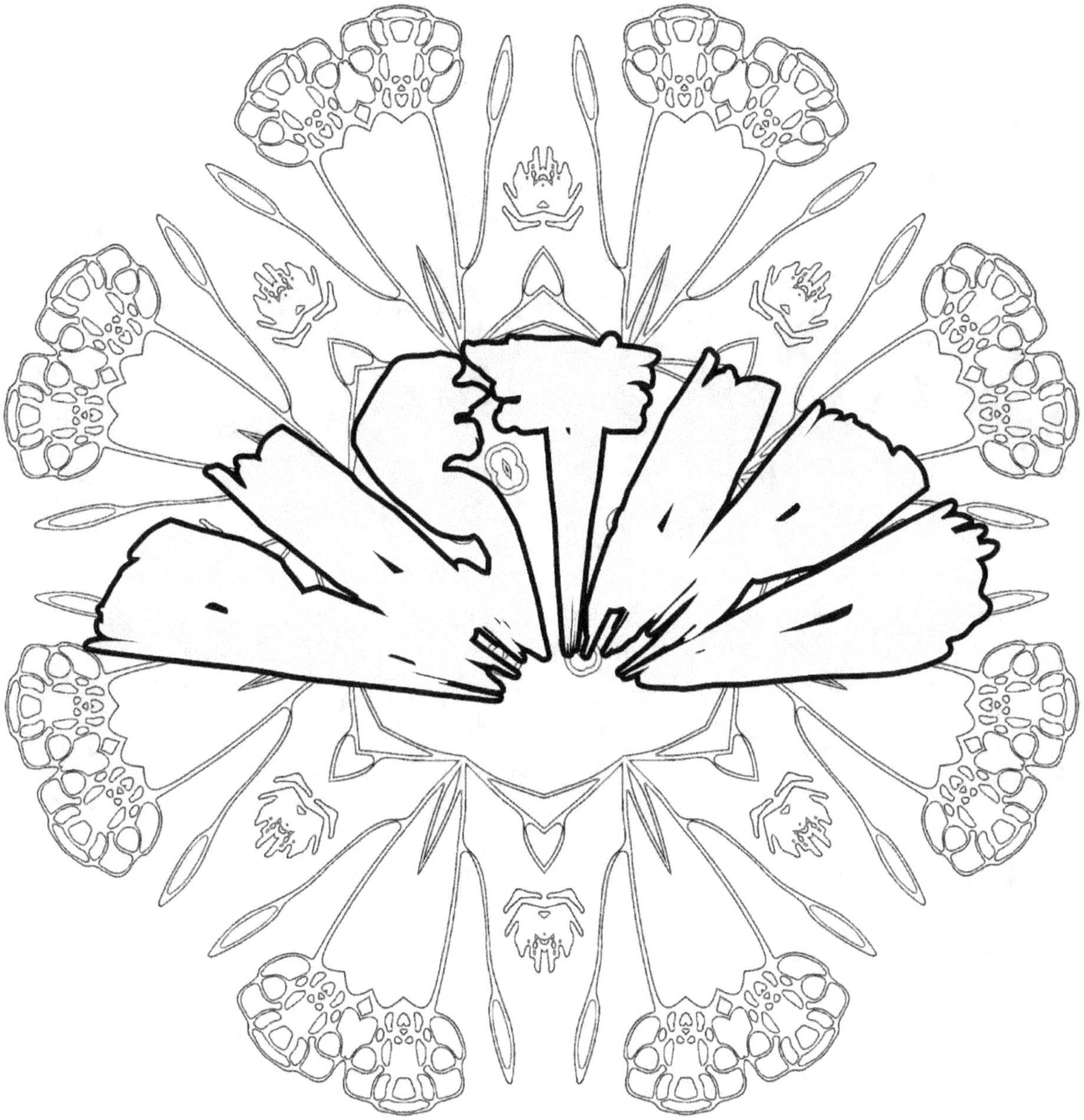

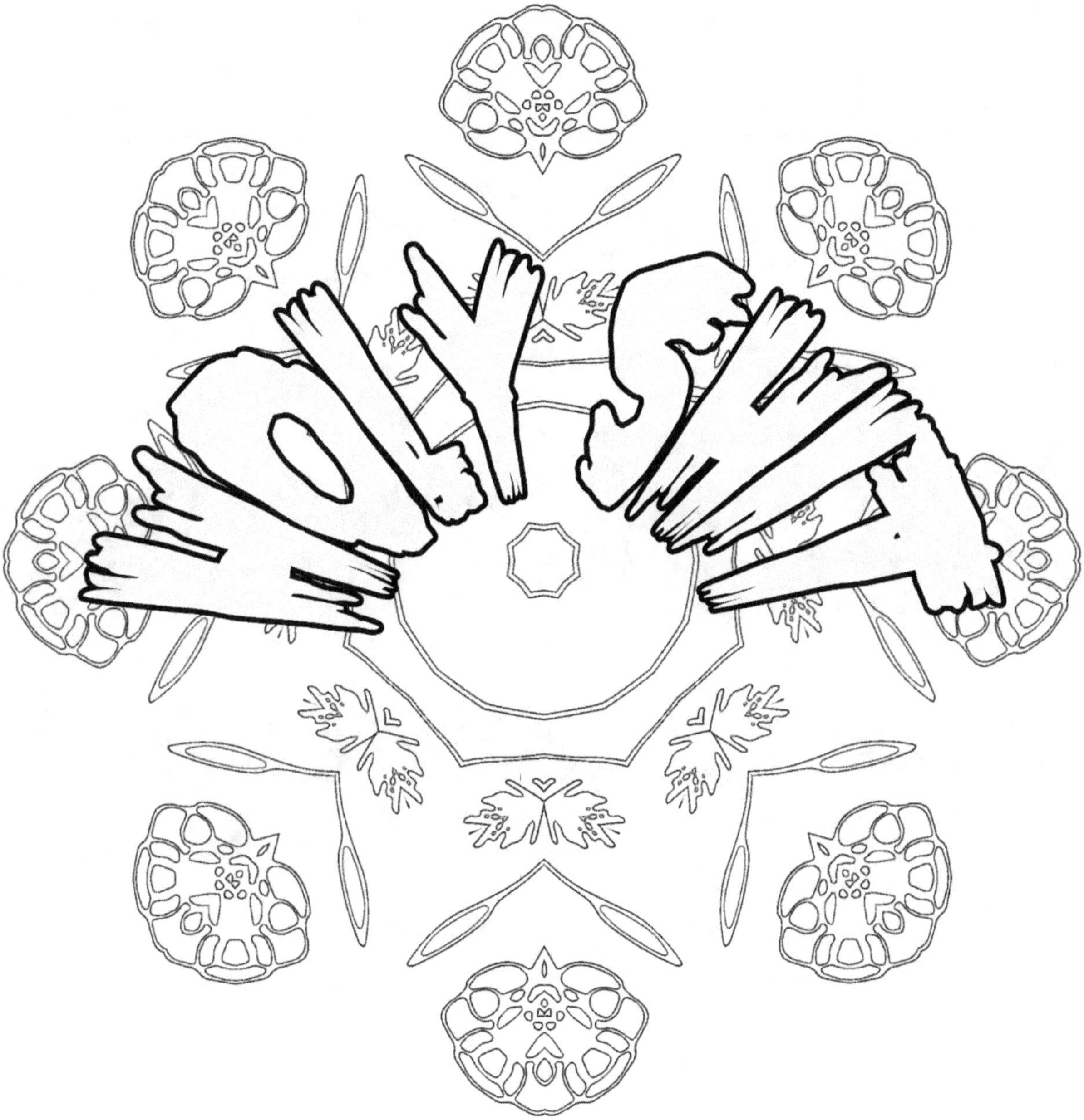
HOLY SHIT

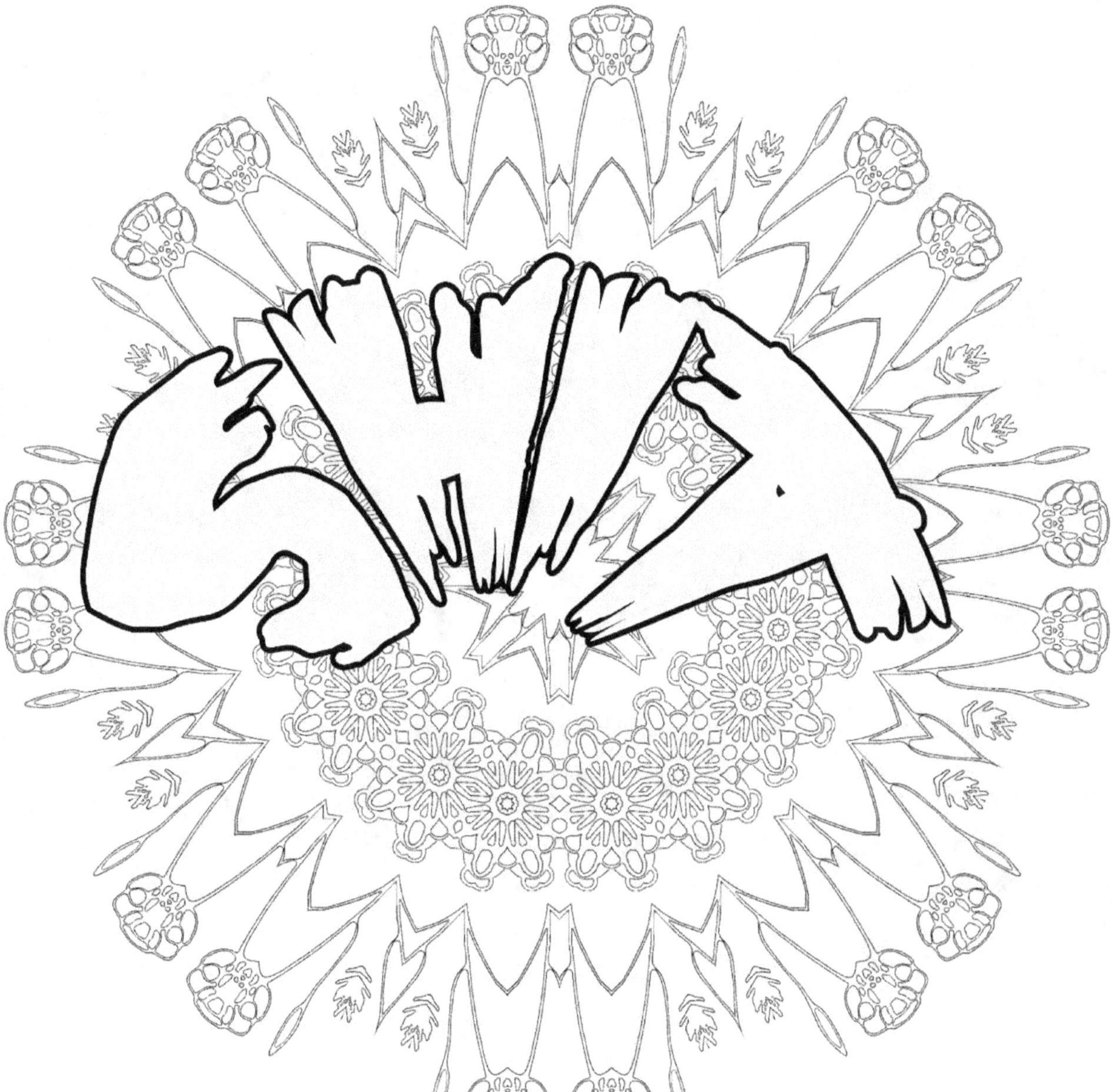

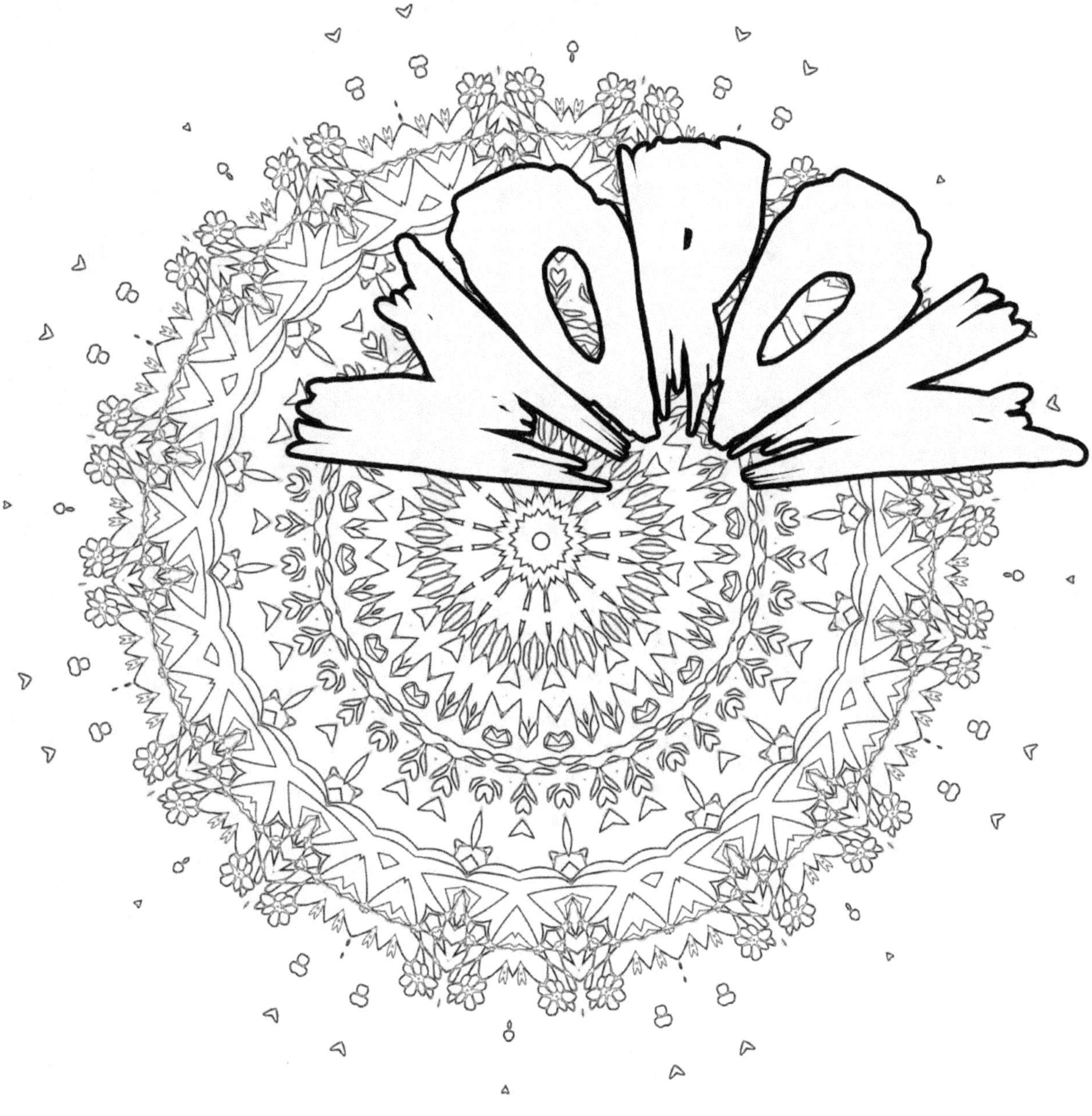

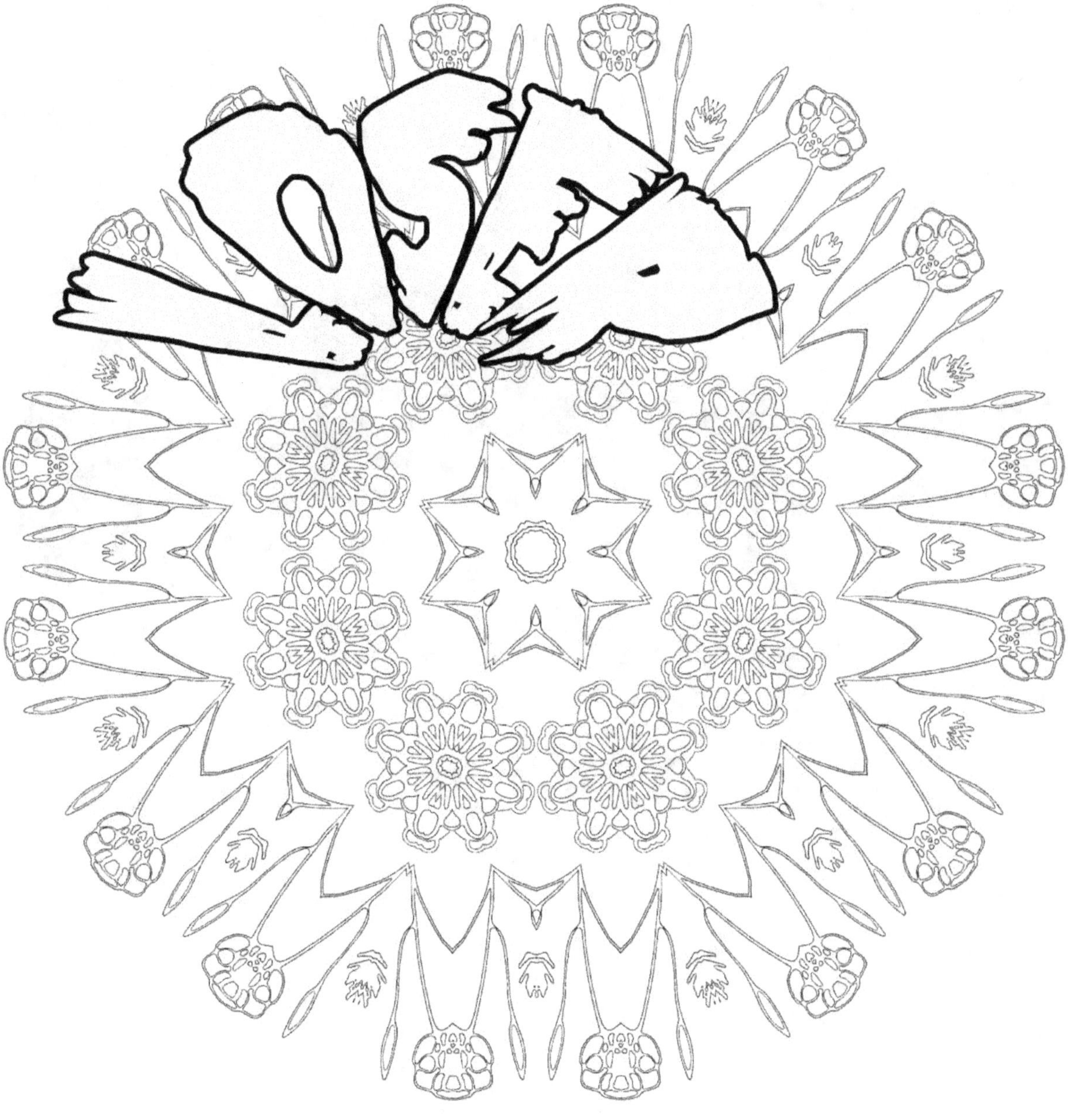

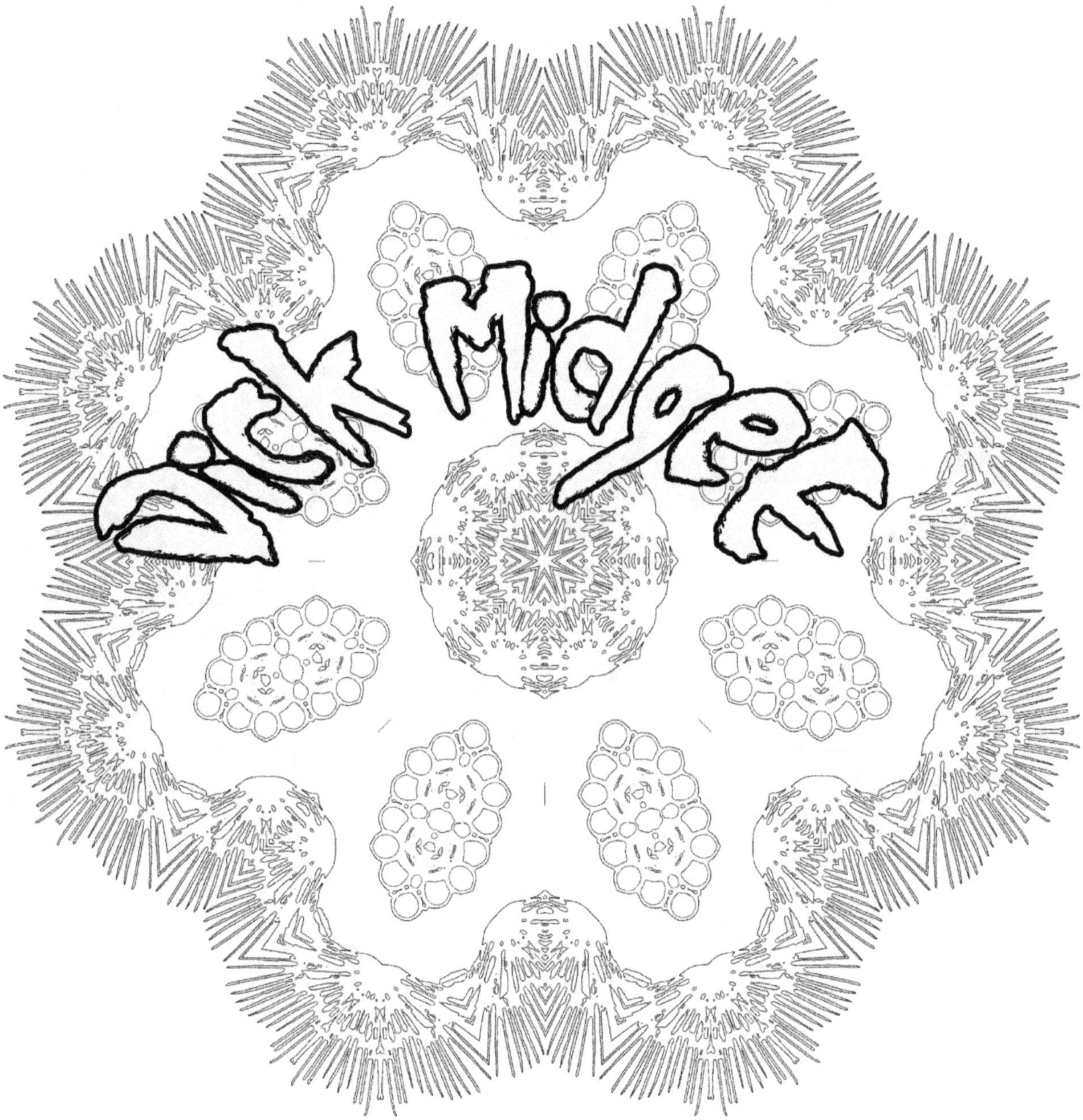
Dick Midget

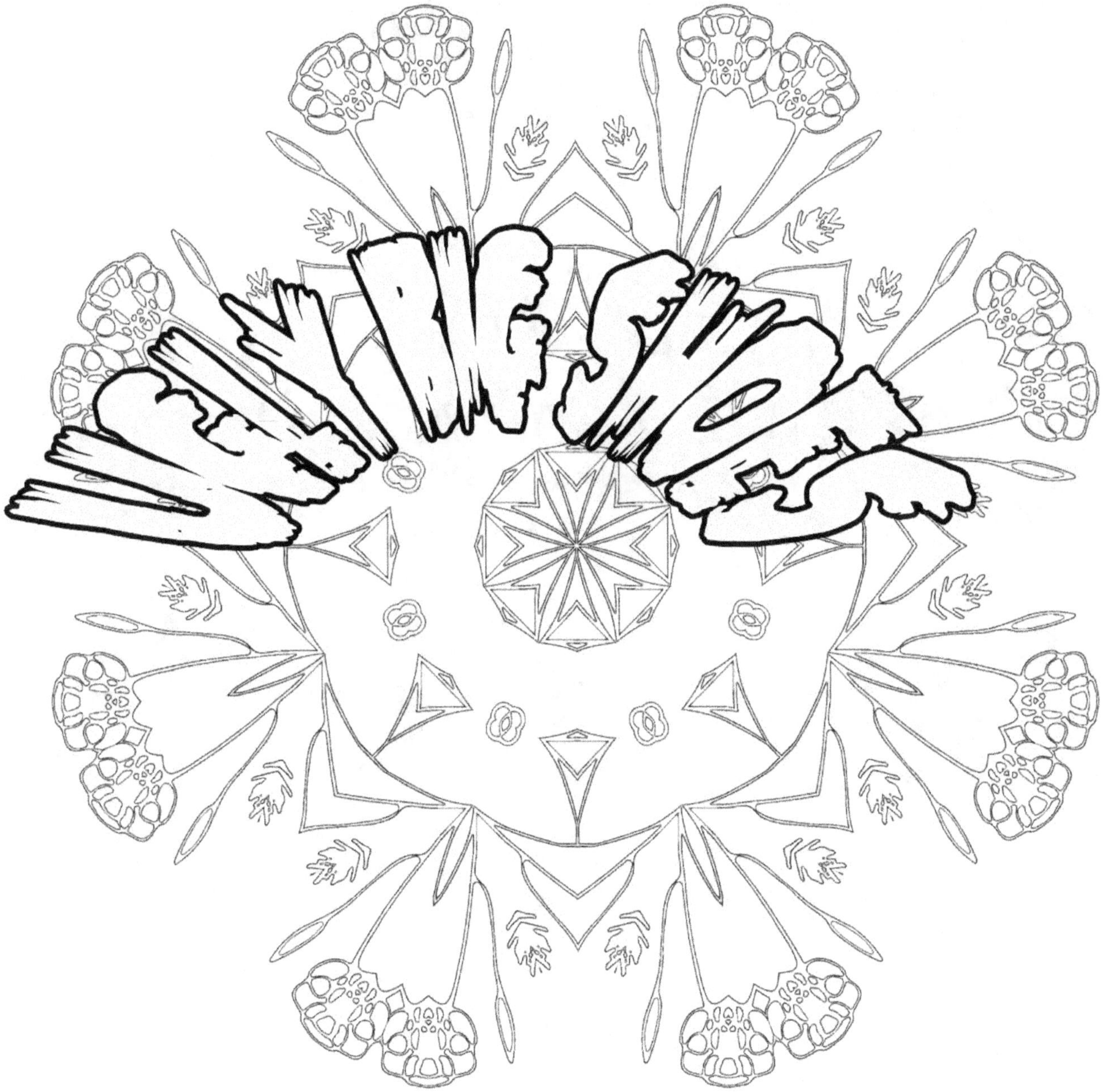
VERY BIG SHOES

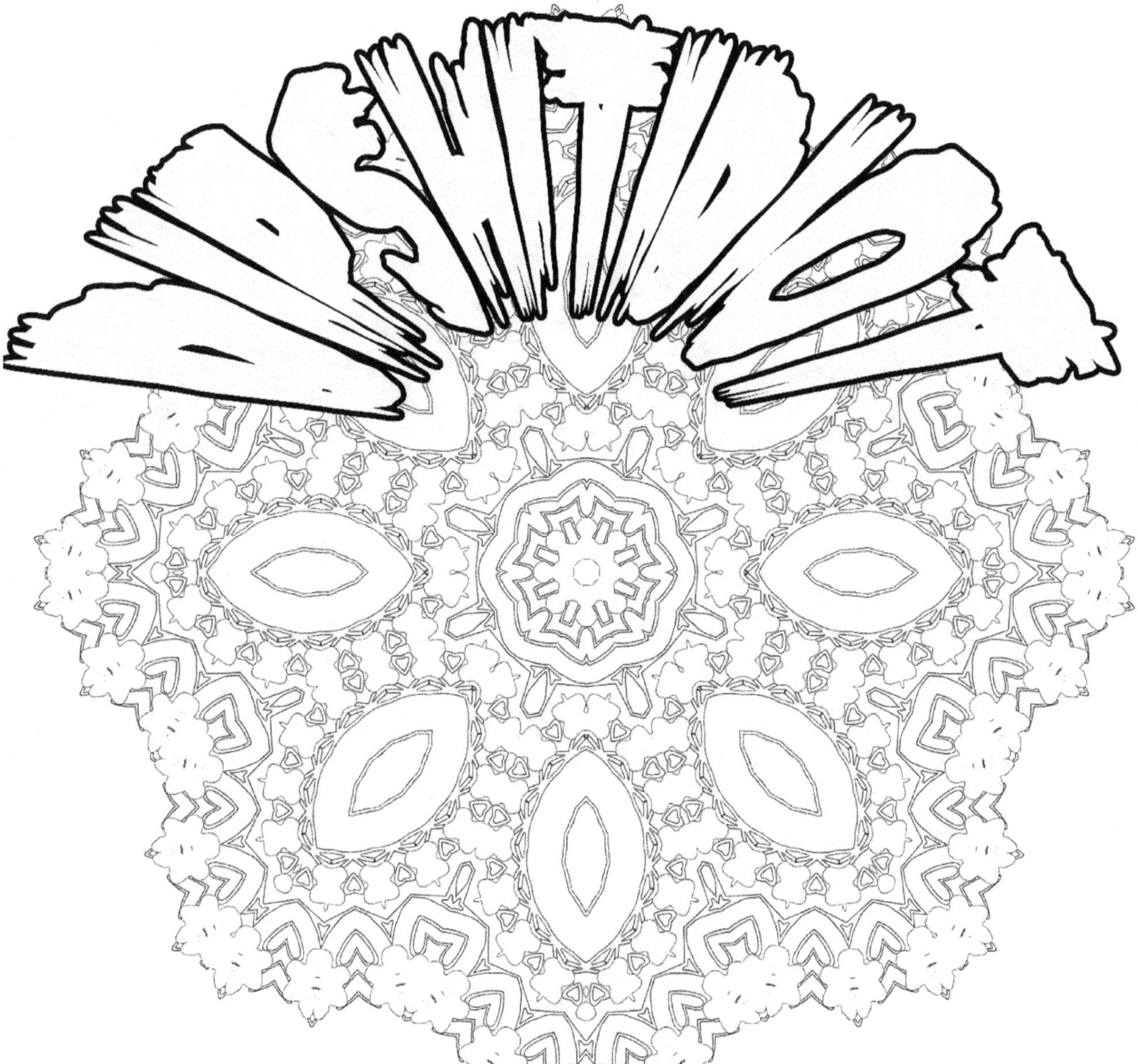

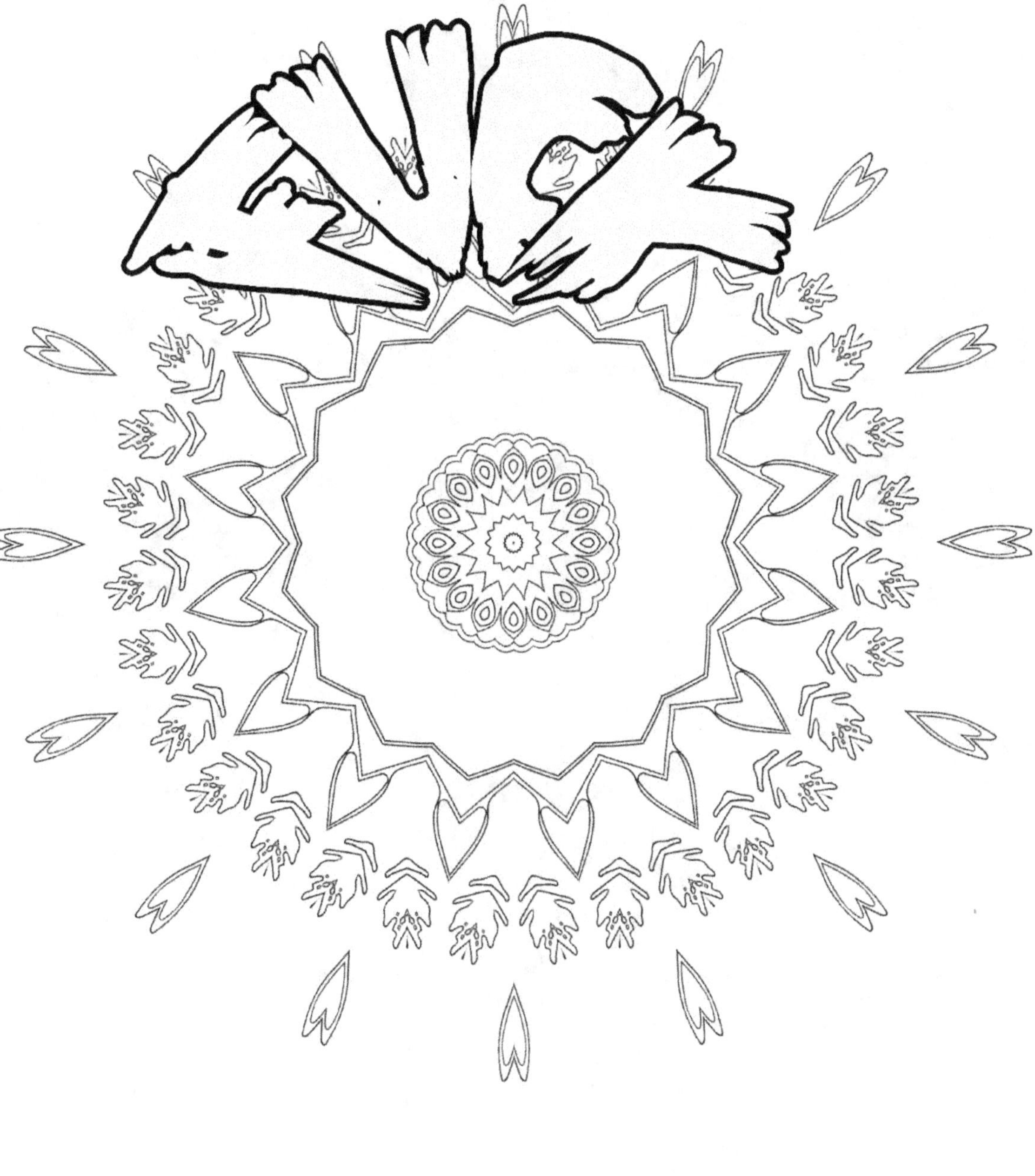

www.ingramcontent.com/pod-product-compliance
Lightning Source LLC
Chambersburg PA
CBHW081745170526
45167CB00009B/3936
* 9 7 8 1 5 4 4 1 8 1 0 6 6 *